Excel Essentials

A Guide for Real-Life Users (Not Technicians!)

Excel Essentials

A Guide for Real-Life Users (Not Technicians!)

By
George W. Rumsey
Computer Resource Center, Inc.
Chicago, Illinois

Published by
Computer Resource Center, Inc.
1525 East 53rd Street, Suite 906
Chicago, IL 60615
Telephone (773) 955-4455
Email gwrumsey@att.net
Web www.computer-resource.com

Excel Essentials

A Guide for Real-Life Users (Not Technicians!)

Basic Spreadsheet Concepts _____ 1
1. The Screen 3
2. Watch the Mouse! 5
3. Getting Around 5
4. Highlighting 6
5. Entering Information 7
6. The Numeric Keypad 7
7. Editing Within a Cell 8
8. Formatting.. 8
9. File 10
10. Document Views 11

Formulas and Functions _____ 12
1. Formulas 12
2. Nesting Operations.. 12
3. Functions.. 13
4. Formula Auditing.. 16
5. Some Commonly Used Functions 17
6. Absolute Cell Addresses 19
7. Links 20
8. Copying or Linking to Word 22

Charting _____ 23
1. Manipulating an Existing Chart 23
2. Chart Tools: Design.. 24
3. Chart Tools: Format 25
4. Sparklines.. 26

Printing _____ 27
1. Print Settings 27
2. Print Preview 27
3. Quick Print.. 30

Page Layout _____ 31
1. Themes 31
2. Page Setup 31
3. Other Page Options 32

Data Tools _____ 33

1. Sort 33
2. Filter 35
3. Text to Columns...37
4. Remove Duplicates and Consolidate....................38
5. Data Validation 40
6. What-If Analysis...41

Subtotals and Group/Ungroup _____ 45

Pivot Tables _____ 48

1. Create a PivotTable 48
2. Modifying Reports 50
3. Formatting...50
4. Pivot Charts 51

More Functions _____ 52

1. Date and Time Functions 52
2. Text Functions 53
3. VLookup and HLookup..56
4. Logical Functions..58

Protecting a Worksheet _____ 59

Excel Keyboard Shortcuts _____ 60

Index of Key Terms_____ 61

Preface

This instructional manual is not an exhaustive guide to Microsoft Excel. Rather, it is a compass, directing you toward key concepts, terms, and commands you need to learn to use Excel effectively and navigate spreadsheets efficiently. It is geared towards users of Excel 2010 and Excel 2013/365.

It also is not intended for a technical audience. I've tried to keep explanations and examples fairly simple and straightforward, and not speak in "computerese" as much as possible. Forgive my lapses, because it is difficult to avoid.

I hope you find this manual useful. Remember "rule number one": *the only way to learn how to use a computer is to use a computer.*

George

Basic Spreadsheet Concepts

Let's start from the beginning: Excel is a spreadsheet. A spreadsheet is a worksheet arranged in columns and rows, and can be used for typing in words and numbers, for organizing and for calculating. For decades, business accountants would create corporate spreadsheets to calculate income and expense, and whether or not you made any money. Today we do such tasks via computer spreadsheet software, which provides you with the worksheet.

A "worksheet" to Excel begins with columns; columns come first and take priority. There are 16,384 columns to each Excel worksheet, identified from A to Z, then from AA to ZZ, and then from AAA through XFD.

Second in order of priority are rows, which are referred to by number. An Excel worksheet provides you with 1,048,576 rows. If you want more, you can have as many additional "sheets" as you need (creating a "workbook").

Where the rows cross the columns, the resulting block is called a "cell." Cells are the tools that do most of the work in Excel. Each cell has name, called the "cell address," consisting of the column letter and the row number:

	A	B	C	D
1	A1	B1	C1	
2			C2	
3			C3	D3
4				

Figure 1 - Spreadsheet Cells

A cell can contain five kinds of content:
- Text (aligns left to right)
- Numbers (aligns right to left)
- Formats (such as $1,000.00 or 2/15/05 or 27.5%)
- Formulas (that do basic math and that you manually type in)
- Functions (more complex calculations and operations that Excel performs for you).

Text is anything that is not purely a number. "27a" is text; so is "60637-1234." So when you are entering *numbers,* type only numbers (not $ or , or %)—those are *formats,* and are usually best applied once your data have been entered and edited. Remember also to *never* use spaces (blank spacebars) in numbers, formulas, or functions.

A *formula* (also called an equation) adds, subtracts, multiplies, or divides; it can use numbers or cells addresses or both. It *always* begins with an equal sign (=), and then shows the operation to be performed. For example, =27+36+99+18 yields the result 180. A formula can also be based on cell addresses (*such as* =a1+a2+a3–d27). Formulas recognize the following symbols:

+ Addition
− Subtraction
* Multiplication
/ Division
^ Exponent, or power

In a formula, always remember the Order of Mathematical Operation, or PEMDAS (Please Excuse My Dear Aunt Sally):

() Parentheses
^ Exponent
* Multiplication
/ Division
+ Addition
- Subtraction

A formula such as =2+3*4 would result in 14; multiplication takes precedence over addition, according to the order of math. But the formula =(2+3)*4 would result in 20.

Many people (including Microsoft) confuse the terms *formula* and *function.* But they are different and don't work the same way.

A *function* is an operation Excel performs for you; it *always* begins with an equal sign (=), followed by a named command (such as "sum" or "average"), a set of parentheses ( ) defining the area to be used, and a cell range (such as a1:a200)—which Excel calls the "argument." For example, the function =average(a1:d1) would return the average of all numbers in cells a1, b1, c1, and d1. The most commonly used function, "sum" or Σ, is for totals. You never have to type functions—they are on your screen, ready to be clicked on. You will find them on the drop-down for the AutoSum, on the *fx* button on the formula bar, and on the "Formulas" tab of the ribbon.

1. The Screen

The Excel work screen is divided into parts. In the very top upper left corner is the "Quick Access" toolbar (for putting commands you use frequently via the dropdown menu at the end). Then you have the tabbed "**ribbon**": File, Home (common commands), Insert (graphics, pivot tables), Design (fonts and colors) Page Layout (margins, paper size), Formulas (functions), Data (sort and select), Review (track changes), and View (screen layout). These tabs are "grouped" into categories (such as Font or Alignment), which frequently offer expandable dialog boxes with more options.

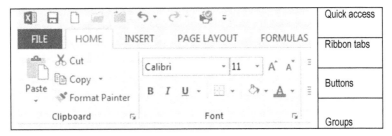

Figure 2 – Quick Access, Ribbon Tabs, and Buttons

Below the ribbon is the most important part of Excel: the "formula bar." The formula bar serves several purposes.

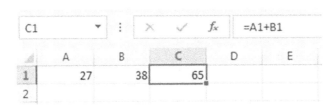

Figure 3 - Formula bar

At the left edge is the cell locator, or "Name Box," where you are currently positioned. A very important rule to always remember in Excel is that *one cell* is always selected—even when you have multiple cells highlighted, one cell is still selected more than the rest, and this is the cell where your results will go. You can also use this cell Name Box to navigate to any cell in your spreadsheet. Click in the Name Box and type in Z5000, press the enter key (return), and you'll move to cell Z5000.

After the Name Box are three buttons. The "X" is the equivalent to cancel (or hitting the ESC key on your keyboard). The check is the equivalent to saying "OK" (you're done). The f_x is a shortcut to the list of Excel functions.

The key part of the Formula Bar is the blank box across the top of your spreadsheet (above the column letters). Another important rule to remember in Excel: the cell shows you what is coming out of your printer, but the Formula Bar shows you what you actually typed. You'll see in Figure 2, that cell C1 contains the number 65; but if you look at the Formula Bar in the example, you'll see that 65 is actually the result of a formula, =A1+B1 (=27+38).

This is also where you edit your information after you've entered it. As you type, you see your data in the cell you have selected, but it also appears on the blank white line of the formula bar.

Below the formula bar is the spreadsheet area (where your mouse appears as a white plus-shape — the cell pointer).

At the bottom left are sheet tabs, where you can add sheets and move to different sheets.

Figure 4 - Sheet Tabs

At the bottom right is a quick view toolbar for adjusting your screen's zoom, as well as page and reading views, along with quick results of any numbers highlighted.

Figure 5 - Status Bar

2. Watch the Mouse!

One of the keys to Excel is paying attention to the mouse. There are many mouse shapes that appear, but four are significant:

 Cell pointer—selects a cell for typing and formatting; highlights an area of cells (range)

 Insertion point—inserts cursor for editing (either by double-clicking a cell or going up to the formula bar and clicking once)

 Move—drag cell contents to different location; this is an alternative to cut and paste for moving cell content from one location to another

 Fill—repeat cell content in either a copy or in a series following a pattern; very useful for repeating formulas and functions

Most of the work you do in Excel involves the cell pointer. It is the shape that selects one cell for typing, or that selects multiple cells for moving, formatting, or printing.

3. Getting Around

Excel provides different ways to navigate around your spreadsheet. A general rule is that the keyboard is always faster, but sometimes the mouse is easier.

By Keyboard:

- **Cursor (arrow)** keys—Move your position up, down, right, and left.
- **ENTER** key—Move your active position down one cell. Shift+enter moves you one row up.
- **TAB** key—Move your active position to the right one column. Shift+tab moves you one cell to the left.
- **F5** (Go To...)—A dialog box opens, in which you can type any cell on the worksheet you want to go to.

By Mouse:

- **Pointer**—Click on any cell where your pointer is, and that becomes your active cell.

- **Scroll Bar**—At the very right side and very bottom of your screen, the scroll bars allow you to move to other areas of your worksheet.
- **Name Box**—In the upper left corner is the box showing your cell location; click in that box, type any cell you would like to go to, then hit enter.

4. Highlighting

The term "highlighting" refers to one of the most basic commands on the computer (not just Excel). It is the command to select an area of your document, in order to carry out specific actions such as cut/copy, format, or print. Excel refers to this as a range of cells. Ranges become important when you work with functions (see below), where they are often part of the "argument."

- To create a range with your mouse, place your cell pointer over a cell, click, hold, and drag the cell down and over until the range you desire is highlighted (or in the opposite direction, if you prefer to work backwards from the bottom up).
- To create a range with your keyboard, move your active cell to the first cell of the intended range, then hold down the SHIFT key and cursor down and over to select the desired range.
- To select an entire column-range or row-range, place the pointer over the column or row headers (the letters or numbers) and click. That entire column or row is selected. To select a bunch of rows or column, click and drag. (Note, this is NOT a good way to format, since you're applying it to millions of cells that will then try to print!)
- To select the entire worksheet, click the blank corner button just above Row 1 and left of Column A.

Noncontiguous Ranges

Ranges where all the cells are adjacent or together as a group are called "contiguous." You can create noncontiguous ranges where the cells that make up that range aren't next to each other. Define your first range as above, then use the mouse to move your cell pointer to the beginning of the second, noncontiguous area. Hold down the CTRL key, and click and drag to select the range. You can do this again and again to select as many noncontiguous ranges as you want, but be careful not to click on a cell without the CTRL key pressed—that deselects all the other ranges.

5. Entering Information

To enter text or numbers, simply select the cell (one click) and start typing. Press enter (return) or tab when done.

When entering text or numbers, if what you type is longer than the cell is wide, one of three things will happen:

- The **text** spills over onto the adjacent cells, because the adjacent cell or cells are empty.
- The **text** is cut off at the end of your cell because the adjacent cell contains text or data, so Excel cannot allow text from one cell to spill onto a cell with something in it.
- Sometimes a **number** in a cell is longer than a cell is wide. When this occurs, you'll see ####### across the cell, indicating you need to widen your cell for the number to appear properly.

Solve this problem by widening your column width (you can't widen just one cell). To widen the column, point your mouse between the two letters at the top of the column and its neighbor; your mouse will turn into a double arrow. Then double-click to adjust the width to "fit to print"—the column becomes the exact width needed to print the content. You can then manually drag an additional distance if you want more space. (Alternatively, go to the button on the ribbon that says "Format" and use the dropdown arrow and select "AutoFit Column Width.")

If you start to type in a cell and change your mind or realize you've made a mistake *and* haven't yet pressed ENTER, you can hit the ESC key or click on the "X" on the formula bar to cancel your typing. If you've hit enter or moved to another cell, and then realize it was a mistake, you can click UNDO from the quick access toolbar.

6. The Numeric Keypad

Many people overlook the keypad on the right-hand side of a standard keyboard (not available on many laptops). The numeric keypad is specifically designed for numerical data entry; most people find it more efficient to type numbers from there. It is particularly useful for quickly accessing +, -, *, and /.

7. Editing Within a Cell

If you move to a cell that already contains content and start to type something in, your new type will completely replace what was there. If you want to edit a cell's contents there are two ways of doing this. *One*, you can move your mouse to the Formula Bar so that the cell pointer becomes the insertion point, then click the mouse to place the cursor in the appropriate area. Like a word processor, you can make any necessary changes with delete and backspace. *Two*, to edit in a cell without going to the Formula Bar, double click in the cell (or hit the F2 Edit key) where you want to make the changes, and the cursor automatically appears in the cell.

> **Excel Tip:** Always be in the cell where you want the answer to appear! As obvious as this may seem, people often write long, complicated formulas and functions in the wrong cells.

8. Formatting

Once all the content is in the worksheet, you'll want to make the sheet look as presentable and as professional as possible. Formatting changes the display of cells, ranges of cells, or the entire worksheet. For instance, you may want a cell or range of cells to reflect currency—so the numbers should have a $ before them; text may look better centered within a cell; subtotals will stick out if the font is larger, bold, or bright blue. You may want some numbers to appear as whole numbers, without decimals. A shaded box around the grand total might be an attention grabber. Formatting allows you to control appearances for when you print. As a general rule, formatting is easiest to apply when you are finished typing and editing.

There are many shortcuts on the ribbon for formatting (be sure to select the cell or range of cells you want to change). The major categories of format are:

- *Font*—Change font, size, or attributes such as bold and italic, and including borders and colors.
- *Alignment*—Determine just how text or numbers align within cells—centered, flush right or flush left, at the top, wrapped, or merged across columns.

- *Number*—Select how that number will appear—with a fixed number of decimals, as a percentage, currency, a date, and many more.
- *Styles*—Choose from pre-defined formats, including conditional formats and cell styles.

If you want more formatting options, go to the dropdown for the various formats on the ribbon. A dialog box will appear with tabbed categories of the types of formatting options available. Here you will find formats for Numbers, Alignment, Font, Border, Fill, and Protection (see page 58).

Conditional Formatting

Conditional Formatting is a command to apply formats based on criteria (such as high to low), and that is tied to the values entered. In the below sample, you can see *Databars* in the number column, *Color Scales* in the cost column, and *Icons* in the total column. You can set your own criteria guidelines by creating a "new rule" (on the dropdown).

	A	B	C	D
1	Date	Number	Cost	Total
2	Monday		27	654 ⬇ $ 17,658
3	Tuesday		89	456 ⬆ $ 40,584
4	Wednesday		65	765 ⬆ $ 49,725
5	Thursday		34	345 ⬇ $ 11,730
6	Friday		23	752 ⬇ $ 17,296
7		Databars	Color Scales	Icons

Figure 6 - Samples of Conditional Formats

Centering Across Columns

To make text or numbers span a series of columns and/or row, you need to use "Merge and Center." First define how wide an area needs to be combined, by highlighting the desired area. Then click on the "Merge and Center" button on the ribbon (under "Alignment").

Do not select any of the three alignment buttons (left, center, right) on the Formatting ribbon—they align text *within* a cell, not *across* cells. And beware, if you highlight multiple cells that have content and then merge, only the first cell's content will remain and the rest will be deleted. Also note that once the cells are merged, you cannot format individual columns; you can "un-merge" the cells if you need to be re-clicking the Merge and Center button.

Excel Tip: One of the most useful shortcuts in Excel for format-ting is the *right mouse button*. The right button gives you the shortcuts for whatever you are pointing at when you right-click. It can be extremely useful for operations such as cut and paste, re-name sheets, insert rows and columns, and even hide or unhide rows or columns for printing.

---

9. File

The "File" tab on the ribbon has gotten very complex over the years. It is still where many of us go (without even thinking) to save or print. But in Excel 2013, you'll have a long list of choices to select from.

- *Info*—Properties about your document, including the "Protect" with password command.
- *New*—Start a new document, either from a blank workbook or from the dozens of free templates provided by Microsoft.
- *Open*—Retrieve an existing document so you can continue working on it. You can open from Recent Workbooks, your Network, your SkyDrive (the online Microsoft cloud), some-where else on your computer, or you can add additional clouds (such as Microsoft SharePoint).
- *"Save" versus "Save as"*—"Save" stores the current document in the "2013" format, asking for a filename that can be up to 256 characters in size (automatically adding a 4-character ex-tension, ".XLSX"). If the document has already been saved, pressing "save" simply resaves it with no questions asked. "Save as" allows you to save a document under a different name (change the name), creating a copy. It gives you an option to specify a different file format (such as "97-03") or a different location. Your locations again include your computer, your network, and your SkyDrive.
- *Print*—This command also includes Print Preview. It lets you adjust your page setup, such as margins, orientation, and scaling (size adjustment).

- *Share*—Share requires you to save your file to a SkyDrive location, then invite people via email to access your file (and even work on it using the online Microsoft Office Web Applications for Word, Excel, and PowerPoint).
- *Export*—Send your workbook to another format, such as PDF.
- *Close*—You're done, you want this document to leave your screen. If you aren't saved, it will prompt you to save before you lose your work.
- *Account*—This screen contains your User Information and your subscription information with Microsoft.
- *Options*—Here you will find all your Excel settings, including options to customize the ribbon and quick access toolbar. If you have difficulty opening files that can be edited, this is also where you find the "Trust Center," where you can tell Excel about your "trusted locations" and how you want downloaded files to open.

To leave the File menu, use the ⬅ symbol at the top of the screen (upper left corner).

10. Document Views

The "View" toolbar (lower right corner, next to the Zoom scale) gives you three different ways to look at your document:

- *Normal*—My "recommended" view, the regular spreadsheet view.
- *Page Layout*—Shows your spreadsheet as individual pages, with margins, headers, and footers (exceptionally useful for creating and editing headers and footers).
- *Page Break Preview*—Shows you how your content is positioned on the pages, and allows you to stretch page size to fit more or less on a page.

To the right of the 3 view buttons is the – and + to control zoom; note this is only a screen view feature, and has no impact on printing.

On the "File" tab under "Print" (and easily added to the Quick Access toolbar, top left) is "print preview."

Formulas and Functions

Formulas and functions are why you use Excel. Microsoft is inconsistent in its application of these terms, but they *are* different. Formulas are more basic, they do what we used to call "arithmetic" (add, subtract, multiply, divide). Functions are more complex, and operate on logical concepts (such as "here ... through ... there"). You manually enter formulas; Excel provides you with the functions. And although you can "add" through the use of either, there are *no* functions that subtract, multiply, or divide.

1. Formulas

Formulas do basic math—add, subtract, multiply, divide. You type them in; Excel never gives you formulas. Formulas can be based on values or on cell addresses, and they always begin with an equal symbol and contain an "operator" such as + or − (plus or minus). =27+3 is a valid formula, as is =a1+b1. Formulas *never* contain a space. If a formula has multiple mathematical operations, then the levels should be separated by parentheses—a step called "nesting."

Excel understands the following operators:

Operator	Purpose	Formula	Answer
+	Addition	=20+7	27
-	Subtraction	=80-6	74
*	Multiplication	=10*34	340
/	Division	=50/5	10
^	Exponentiation	=3^4	81

Excel Tip: For repetitive formulas or functions, use the "Fill" corner and drag to adjoining cells, either horizontally or vertically. This is the best shortcut in Excel!

2. Nesting Operations

When using operators such as + and *, Excel always assumes that multiplication and division take priority over addition and subtraction (see PEMDAS, page 2). Therefore, if you need to add two numbers, then multiply by a third number, you must identify which step to do first by placing it in parentheses.

Formula	Result	Action
=2+4*3	14	This formula multiplies 4*3 (which equals 12), then adds 2.
=(2+4)*3	18	This formula nests 2+4 (6), then multiplies by 3.
=((9-2)/3)+6	8.33	Subtracts 9-2 (7), then divides 7 by 3 (2.33), then adds 6.
=(2+3)^2*4	100	First add 2+3 (5), then square it (25), then multiple times 4 (100).

As you type "nested" formulas, watch the parentheses. You'll see that Excel color-codes each so that you can make sure each opening parenthesis has a corresponding closing parenthesis.

3. Functions

A function is a mathematical or logical operation that Excel provides for you. It contains a name and an "argument." For instance, rather than typing =B5+C5+D5+E5+F5, you might create the function =SUM(B5:F5), where B5:F5 is the argument and SUM is the name. Some arguments are very simple, such as the one for a basic SUM, and others are more complex, as shown on the following pages.

Be careful when selecting functions. There are often many variations of the same function, so use your help screen to make sure you are picking the one that will most accurately do the task you need to accomplish. For example, there is a function called "count" (returns a total of how many numbers you have), but there is also "countA" (how many cells with content, numbers or text), "countBlank" (how many cells are empty), "countIf" (count on a conditional basis, such how many numbers are >25), and even "countIfS" (count on multiple conditions).

Accessing the Functions

Functions are so important and so useful to Excel, they are located all over your screen. If you look at the Home tab on the ribbon, near the right side is the AutoSum (Σ) button; note it has a dropdown, with common functions, and at the bottom, "More Functions." This takes you to the list of recently used functions in the "Insert Function" window.

You can also find the functions on the Formula Bar, on the f_x symbol. Clicking it also brings up the "Insert Function" window. Note that one of your options on the dropdown is "All Functions." The Insert Function window is also particularly useful, since it gives you a mini-help screen that explains what each function does.

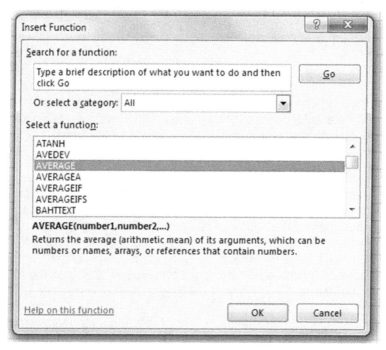

Figure 7 - Insert Function, Set to "All"

If you click in a cell and start typing = followed by a function name, the function list will appear. Double-click any function to select it, and then you can complete its argument.

Perhaps the most thorough way of accessing your functions is on the Formulas tab of the ribbon, where you'll find the Function library. There the functions are separated into categories.

Types of Functions

The Function Library separates the functions into the following categories:

- Recent Used
- Financial

- Logical
- Text
- Date & Time
- Lookup & Reference
- Math & Trig
- More Functions
    o Statistical
    o Engineering
    o Cube
    o Information
    o Compatibility
    o Web

Examples of many of these function categories are included in Section 5 (below).

Using a Function

When you have selected a particular function from the Insert Function window, selecting "OK" takes you to the Argument screen. The Function Argument window will show you what arguments are needed to make the function work; click on each to get an explanation of what is required. At the bottom left corner is a preview of the "Result" based on your current argument. Click OK when satisfied.

Example: Suppose you wanted to calculate the depreciation value of a new computer for your taxes. You would use the Financial function called "DB" (or Declining Balance, since a computer can be amortized or depreciated over time).

For this function, you need to have four arguments:
- *Cost* — the initial cost of the asset (how much did you pay for the computer?)
- *Salvage* — the salvage value at the end of the life of the asset (what would you get if you sold the old computer when it comes time to buy a new computer?)
- *Life*—the number of periods over which the asses is depreciated (or useful life of the asset, usually in years) (how long are you going to be able to use this computer?)
- *Period*—the period for which you want to calculate the depreciation, in the same units as life (which year are you deducting?)

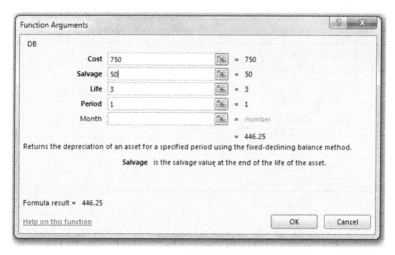

Figure 8 - "Declining Balance" (DB) Function Argument

Note that "Month" at the bottom is not bold, indicating it is not a required field. Depreciation is usually a fiscal year calculation, not based on the particular month.

In this example, when I hit OK, the answer is going to be $446.25 that I can deduct on this year's taxes.

All functions follow these steps. You must
1) Decide which function you need to perform an operation.
2) Understand the argument(s) needed to make the function work.

4. Formula Auditing

On the Formulas tab are some of the most useful commands in Excel. Particularly useful is the "Show Formulas." It allows you to see the actual formulas in each cell—and print them, so you can have a hard copy to refer to. Seeing your formulas is very useful for trouble-shooting error messages, and for formula checking.

"Formula checking" means tracking the sources or results of your calculations. There are two options called "Trace Precedents" and "Trace Dependents." Precedents shows you where a formula or function is pulling its data; Dependents show you cells that would change as a result of changing that cell. In Figure 6, cell B2 has two dependents (D2 and B7); cell D7 has 5 precedents (d2 through d6).

	A	B	C	D
1	Date	Number	Cost	Total
2	Monday	27	654	=B2*C2
3	Tuesday	89	456	=B3*C3
4	Wednesday	65	765	=B4*C4
5	Thursday	34	345	=B5*C5
6	Friday	23	752	=B6*C6
7	Total	=SUM(B2:B6)	=SUM(C2:C6)	=SUM(D2:D6)
8				

Figure 9 - Show Formulas, with Auditing Arrows

The arrows stay visible (and print) until you click the button "Remove Arrows." Formulas stay visible and print until you turn off the "Show Formulas" button.

5. Some Commonly Used Functions

Function	Explanation and Example	Result
AVEDEV	Average Deviation of data points from the mean; a measure of the variability in a data set; can contain numbers of cells.	
	=AVEDEV(13,19,27,33)	7
AVERAGE	Average of the data set; contains numbers or cells.	
	=AVERAGE(13,19,27,33)	23
CONCATENATE	Joins several text cells into one	
	=CONCATENATE(A1,", B1")	Smith, Joe
COUNT	Count how many **numbers** are in a range of cells.	
	=COUNT(A1:D4)	2
COUNTA	Count how many nonblank values (cells with contents, either text or numbers) are in a range of cells.	
	=COUNTA(A1:D4)	13
COUNTIF	Count how many numbers are in a range, based on a criteria	
	=COUNTIF(A1:D4>10)	5
DATE	Returns the "serial number" of a particular date (the numeric value to Excel of that date); contains year, month, date.	
	=DATE(96,12,25)	35424
DATEVALUE	The "serial number" of the date used to convert a date typed as text into the numeric value (useful within other functions).	
	=DATEVALUE("8/16/96")	35293

Function	Explanation and Example	Result
DAYS360	Results in the number of days between two dates based on a 360-day year, useful for accounting systems based on twelve 30-day months; contains the start date and end date.	
	=DAYS360("1/1/96","1/1/97")	360
DB	Depreciation of an asset for specified time, with fixed-declining balance; *cost* is initial cost, *salvage* is value at end, *life* is number of periods being depreciated, *period* is year to calculate.	
	DB(cost,salvage,life,period) =DB(1000,50,5,1) ($1,000 cost, resale $50, 5 years, first year)	$451.00
FREQUENCY	Frequency distribution of a range of values, at specified intervals (a second range of values called "bins").	
	FREQUENCY(range,bins)	
FV	Future value of an investment based on periodic, constant payments and constant interest rate; *rate* is the interest rate per period, *nper* is the total number of payment periods, *pmt* is the payment per period.	
	=FV(0.08125/12,24,100)	($2,596.49)
HOUR	Shows the value of an hour of day.	
	=HOUR("3:30 pm")	15
IF	Returns one value if logical test is true and another if false; *logical test* is an instruction, such as > or <, *value_if_true* or *value_if_false* is a value to report if true (or false).	
	IF(logical test,value_if_true, value_if_false) =IF(d13>10,"wow","oops")	wow
IPMT	Interest payment for a specified period of time based on periodic, constant payments and constant interest; *rate* is interest per period, *per* is the period you want the interest for, *nper* is total number of payments, *pv* is the present value.	
	IPMT(rate,per,nper,pv) IPMT(0.08125/12,1,360,93600)	($633.75)
MAX	Maximum value in a range.	
	MAX(d1:d15)	35424
MEDIAN	Number in the middle of a set of cells.	
	MEDIAN(d1:d15)	14
MIN	Shows minimum value in a range of cells.	
	MIN(d1:d15)	-2596.49
MODE	Most frequently occurring value in a range of data.	
	MODE(5,9,4,5,3,2,6,1,5,9)	5
NOW	Serial number of the current date and time; updates when document is used.	
	NOW()	2/4/2014 16:16
PI	Inserts the value of PI, to 15 digits.	
	PI()	3.141592654
PMT	Periodic payment for an annuity, based on constant interest rate, number of payments, and present value.	
	PMT(rate,nper,pv) PMT(0.08125/12,360,93600)	($694.98)

Function	Explanation and Example	Result
PROPER	Converts text to "Proper" case (see also Upper and Lower)	
	=PROPER(A1)	Brown, Mary
PPMT	Payment on principal for a given period, based on rate, period to be calculated, number of payments, and present value.	
	PPMT(rate,per,nper,pv) PPMT(0.08125/12,1,360,93600)	($61.23)
PV	Present value of an investment, based on rate, number of payments, and payment each period.	
	PV(rate,nper,pmt) PV(0.08125/12,360,700)	($94,276.45)
ROUND	Rounds a number to a specified number of digits.	
	ROUND(2.149,1)	2.1
STDEV	Estimate for the standard deviation based on a range of cells.	
	STDEV(d1:d25)	26086.62
TIME	Serial number of a particular time, in hours, minutes, seconds.	
	TIME(16,45,15)	4:45 PM
TODAY	Returns the serial number of the current date.	
	TODAY()	2/4/2014

6. Absolute Cell Addresses

When using commands such as "Copy" or "Fill" to move or repeat functions, you have to remember that cell addresses change when they are moved; for example, if you shift a formula in C1 that reads =a1+b1 to the cell D1, it will change automatically to read =b1+c1—since C1 became D1, then A1 becomes B1, and B1 becomes C1.

To prevent cells in formulas from shifting, you can "lock" a cell address by making it *absolute*. Absolute cells are identified by the $ symbol: $B1 locks the column; B$1 locks the row; $B$1 locks both column and row. This is especially useful in calculating complex formulas, such as percentages, where the total is in B4:

	A	B	C	Formula	Result
1	Jan	43	48.31	=(B1/$B$4)	Divide 43 by 89 (the total)
2	Feb	34	38.20	=(B2/$B$4)	Divide 34 by 89 (still the total)
3	Mar	12	13.48	=(B3/$B$4)	Divide 12 by the total
4	Total	89	100.00	=SUM(C1:C3)	Sum 48.31+38.20+13.48

Excel Tip: The shortcut key for making a cell absolute is F4. If you press it once, you lock both column and row, press again to lock just the column, press again to lock just the row, press a fourth time to unlock the formula.

7. Links

There are three kinds of data links in Excel: linking across sheets (same file), linking across files (different workbooks), and linking to other programs (such as Word).

Linking across Sheets and Workbooks

To copy data from one workbook to another is pretty straightforward; simply highlight the source data, select Copy, then toggle to another workbook file (use Alt+Tab or the Windows task bar at the bottom of the screen), then Paste. However, when you try to cut or copy formulas, you often will get errors (such as "#REF"), because Excel always adjust formulas and functions to match the new locations. In the sample below, look what happens when I copy Colum D in Sheet 1 and paste it to Column B in Sheet 2.

	A	B	C	D
1	first quarter report			
2	staff	income	expense	balance
3	Alice	799.00	114.50	684.50
4	Bob	756.00	341.00	415.00
5	Carol	847.00	287.00	560.00
6	Ted	813.00	395.00	418.00
7	Total	$3,215.00	$1,137.50	$2,077.50
8				

	A	B	C
1	Annual Report		
2	staff	1st Qtr	
3	Alice	#REF!	
4	Bob	#REF!	
5	Carol	#REF!	
6	Ted	#REF!	
7	Total	#REF!	

Figure 10 - Error Message from Failed Copy

⋈	A	B	C	D
1	first qua			
2	staff	income	expense	balance
3	Alice	799	114.5	=B3-C3
4	Bob	756	341	=B4-C4
5	Carol	847	287	=B5-C5
6	Ted	813	395	=B6-C6
7	Total	=SUM(B3:B6)	=SUM(C3:C6)	=B7-C7
8				

⋈	A	B
1	Annual Repc	
2	staff	1st Qtr
3	Alice	=#REF!-A3
4	Bob	=#REF!-A4
5	Carol	=#REF!-A5
6	Ted	=#REF!-A6
7	Total	=#REF!-A7
8		

Figure 11 - Illegal References Caused by Copy

(The first views are the original sheets, the second is with "Show Formulas" turned on). Look at the formula in cell D3, and then see what happened when it copies to the next sheet's cell B3. C3 on sheet one became A3 on sheet 2; B3 on sheet one became "Invalid Reference" on sheet 2. Everything was adjusted by two columns, since it was copied from D to B (and there aren't two columns before B, hence the invalid reference!).

There are a couple of ways around this problem. In Excel, when you paste (after a cut or copy), you will find a very useful dropdown on the "Paste" button (on the "Home" tab), which gives you options as to how your paste should occur. The bottom option called "Paste Special" spells out the choices:

- *Formulas*—Paste the formulas (which usually will mess up if across sheets or files).
- *Values*—Paste the results, not the formulas.
- *Formats*—Paste just the formats, not the content.

- *Comments*—Paste any inserted notes.
- *Validation*—Paste only data that pass a certain criteria (such as numbers >25).
- *All using Source theme*—Paste fonts, colors, effects.
- *All except borders*—Don't include borders in paste.
- *Column widths*—Only paste the column width.
- *Formulas and number formats*—Paste formatted formulas.
- *Values and number formats*—Paste formatted values.
- *All merging conditional formats*—Paste with conditional formats.
- *Skip blanks*—Paste, eliminating blanks.
- *Transpose*—Switch rows to columns, or columns to rows.
- *Paste Link*—Establish a connection across sheets, so that if one changes, the other updates automatically.

The best choices on this list are to paste Values, Values and Number Formats, and Paste Link. "Paste Link" will maintain a relationship between the two tables. That is, if the source cell in the source worksheet changes, the linked cell in the linked sheet will change accordingly.

8. Copying or Linking to Word

You can copy worksheet contents to a Microsoft Word document quite easily. Highlight a cell or range of cells in Excel, choose Copy (Ctrl+C, right-click, or use the Copy button on the ribbon), then toggle to Word. Place your cursor where you want to insert the worksheet data, then simply choose Paste. The values of your data will appear in Word's Table format.

But perhaps a better option is to use Paste Special, where you will find a "Link" option (be sure to select that it is a link to Microsoft Excel Worksheet Object). Tables that are linked from Word back to Excel can only be updated or edited in Excel. If you need to email someone the Word document, the Excel link will not update and cannot be edited unless you also send them the Excel worksheet (unless the link is to a file that is on a shared network drive).

This command works with graphs as well as with worksheets.

Charting

An Excel chart is based on numerical data you wish to graph. The key to charting is properly selecting the correct data to be included in the graph. Once selected (remember to use CTRL to skip portions, and you usually don't include totals), click the Insert tab on the ribbon and pick your chart type (column, line, pie, bar, area, scatter, other). This automatically inserts the chart into your sheet, as well as adds new tabs to the ribbon for *Chart Tools* (Design and Format).

1. Manipulating an Existing Chart

To manipulate a chart, you first select it. To do this, simply place your mouse pointer anywhere in the chart and click once. Graphical "handles" should appear on the chart edges.

You will also see a small toolbar appear at the right side of the chart, with three buttons. The + symbol gives a list of chart elements; the paintbrush is chart style and color; and the filter shows the data source (all of these options are repeated on the Design and Format tabs on the ribbon).

Moving and Sizing a Chart

With the chart active, point the mouse at the frame or border outlining the chart, then click and drag, moving the mouse, and the chart moves with you. Note there is also a button on the ribbon called "Move Chart," which lets you shift the chart to a new sheet (while keeping it linked to the data).

To enlarge, shrink, or change the size of the chart, place the pointer on any of the "handles" on the frame until the pointer's shape changes into double-arrows, then click and drag. The outline you draw will change the chart accordingly. Corner handles enlarge and shrink; center and middle handles stretch.

Formatting

Clicking once on a chart allows you to move the chart or change the dimensions. But you may want to change other aspects of the chart as well. If you point at any specific section of the chart (such as a slice of the pie or the label on an axis) and then double-click, you'll have a new window on the right of your screen for "Formatting. The choices that show up reflect the chart part you clicked on. (These same choices are on the ribbon for Chart Tools/Format, Current Selection.)

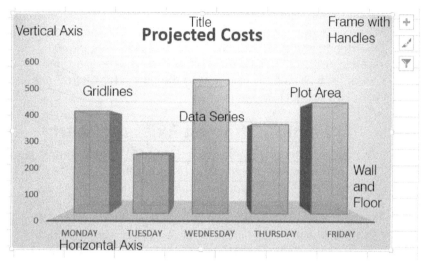

Figure 12 - Parts of a Chart

Deselecting

After completing your chart changes, simply "Click Away"—or click anywhere on the worksheet outside the chart frame. This turns off all parts of the chart and removes the chart tools from the ribbon.

2. Chart Tools: Design

- *Add Chart Element*—Add (or remove) chart titles, data labels, data table, legend, lines, trend lines, and up/down bars. Available choices depend on the type of chart you are working with (pie charts, for example, do not have trend lines).
- *Quick Layout*—Multiple designs for layout, affecting the position, size, and visibility of different chart elements (such as labels or axes).
- *Change Colors*—Different color combinations, based on your "Theme" colors.

- *Chart Styles*—This option is an "expander" (see the drop-down arrow in the bottom right corner). When expanded, there are multiple layouts for each chart type, impacting the title, legend, axes, gridlines, and more.
- *Switch Row/Column*—Flip the display of your data: switch x axis to y, and vice-versa. Changes the display and the formats.
- *Select Data*—Re-select data to be included in the chart. Use this if you did not correctly select your data at the beginning.
- *Chart Type*—Opens the dialog window that allows you to select the kind of chart you wish to have (column, line, pie, bar, area, XY, stock, surface, doughnut, bubble, radar). There are multiple designs for each chart type; for example, for column charts, there are side-by-side, stacked, percentile, and front-to-back.
- *Location: Move Chart*—This command allows you to move the chart from an embedded-in-the-spreadsheet object (which often means it is difficult to print in an attractive way) to a separate, new sheet (its own worksheet). Having a chart on a linked worksheet often makes editing and formatting (and printing!) much easier.

3. Chart Tools: Format

- *Current Selection*—First single left-click on the portion of the chart you would like to change. The part you click on appears in the top drop-down of this group. There is both a "format" command and a reset command.
- *Insert Shapes*—Allows you to insert a shape or text box into the chart area.
- *Shape Styles*—Predesigned or custom fills, outlines, and effects for the components of the chart (such as fill colors or borders or shadows).
- *Word Art Styles*—Predesigned or custom text formats (including text color, text border, and text effects such as glow).
- *Arrange*—Bring to front or send to back (used when there are multiple objects embedded within a chart.
- *Size*—The horizontal and vertical dimensions of your chart. This is an alternative way of sizing, as opposed to dragging handles.

4. Sparklines

Sparklines are a different kind of chart, which is embedded within a cell. It is meant to give a quick visual summary (a "trend"), without having to actually create a chart. There are three kinds of sparklines: line, column, and win/loss. They are tied to the original numbers, and re-draw when the data change.

To create a Sparkline, first select the cell where you want the graph to go. Then click the Sparkline button for Line, column, or Win/Loss. A window pops up, asking you to define your data range (by highlighting or selecting the data you want to use in your sparkline); it also shows you the cell where the sparkline will be positioned. Clicking OK inserts the Sparkline onto your spreadsheet.

Once the Sparkline has been inserted, you'll find a new tab on the ribbon for "Sparkline Tools / Design." This gives you the ability to edit your data, switch between the different types, highlight high and low points (or first and last points, negative points, or marker points), and format colors and line thicknesses.

January	15%
February	-12%
March	48%
Line	
Column	
Win/Loss	

Figure 13 - Sparklines

Printing

The Print command (located on the "File" tab of the ribbon) allows you to print the entire spreadsheet, the entire workbook (all sheets), the highlighted (selected) area, or page ranges (such as 2 to 4). It also gives you a "Print Preview" so you can see what your document will look like when it prints and how it fits on the page.

When you go to the File/Print command, at the top of the screen is the "Print" button and the number of copies; below that is the default printer, with a dropdown if you have multiple printers to choose from. Then you see "Settings."

1. Print Settings

- *Page Active Sheets*—Allows you to select what you want to print: entire sheet, entire workbook (multiple sheets), high-lighted area, or specific pages.
- *Print One Sided*—Available if your printer can do duplex (front-to-back) printing.
- *Collated*—If you are printing more than one copy, you can specify how your pages are organized.
- *Orientation*—Portrait or landscape printing.
- *Paper Size*—Letter, legal, or other.
- *Normal Margins*—Set your print margins.
- *Scaling*—Enlarge or shrink your document to fit a specific number of pages.
- *Page Setup*—This command has some of the most useful functions for printing, including printing the gridlines, page numbers, and headers and footers. This option also allows you to center your table on the page, and to shrink or enlarge your table. See Page Layout for details.

2. Print Preview

Automatically showing on the print menu is "Print Preview," which shows you how your document will print based on the current Print Settings. At the bottom is a scroll bar for moving through pages (if more than one page). In the lower right corner of the preview screen are two buttons, one to activate margins and one to control zoom (to enlarge or shrink your screen view, with no impact on the printout).

Page

- *Orientation*—Do you want to print your worksheet like a letter ("portrait" or "tall") or on its side ("landscape" or "wide")?
- *Scaling*—Very cool stuff! Allows you to shrink or enlarge the contents of your worksheet on the paper. For example: Let's say you have a worksheet that fits on two pages, but you want to see it on one. Simply select the Fit to: button, and make sure it's 1 page wide by 1 page tall. All on one page! Warning! Don't try to scale a 50-page worksheet to one page. It is unreadble, and you might well freeze (crash) the computer or worse.
- *Paper Size*—Allows you to decide what size paper you'll be printing on.
- *Print Quality*—Determines the resolution of the printout in DPI (dots per inch, such as 600 DPI or 1200 DPI).
- *1st Page*—What number to start numbering with.
- *Options...*—Allows you configure how your printer will print, such as print quality (DPI) or duplex (front and back).

Margins

This command sets page margins for printing, and the areas in which headers and footers will fit. It also allows you to center your worksheet both horizontally and vertically on the page. (Try this when working on small worksheets.)

Headers/Footers

Headers are text that repeats at the top of every page. Footers are the same, except they're at the bottom of every page. The boxes display the current settings, which are usually blank. There are a number of quick-to-use built-in headers and footers on the drop-down below Header or Footer, respectively.

If you want to *really* customize your headers/footers, select the "Custom Header" (or Footer) button. This brings up a toolbar and, below that, three boxes, labeled Left, Center, and Right Sections. This displays what appears in the Headers and Footers. You can type text in these Section boxes as well as insert various codes.

- The "A" button allows you to select the fonts, styles and sizes to be used.
- The "#" button will insert a code that will display the current page.

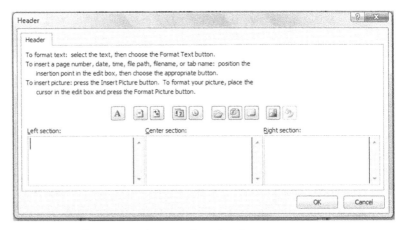

Figure 14 - Custom Header Screen

- The "+ +" button inserts a code displaying the total number of pages in the worksheet.
- The Calendar button displays the print date.
- The Clock button inserts the print time.
- The yellow folder button inserts the file path (such as c:/users/documents/work).
- The green Excel logo button displays the filename.
- The sheet button displays the sheet (tab) name.
- The mountain button allows you to insert a graphic (such as a logo).
- The final button (grayed out unless you have a graphic) is to format the picture (such as size).

Sheet

- *Print Area*—Displays the range selected to print.
- *Print Titles*—If you have column headings you want repeated every page (similar to a Header, but different), select specific rows or columns to repeat. (Note: This does *not* work in Print Preview / Page Setup; it does work on the Page Layout tab. Stupid Microsoft programming....)
- *Print: Gridlines*—Selects or deselects the gridlines (does not affect the monitor display).
- *Comments*—To print comments or notes within the document.
- *Black & White*—Prints with no color or gray scale.

- *Draft Quality*—Tells the printer to use less ink (so you don't waste expensive color toner).
- *Row & Column Headings*—If you want A,B,C column headings and 1,2,3 row headings to appear.
- *Page Order*—Determines how the multiple pages will print (down and across, or across and down—that is, which direction is page 2? Is it from left to right, then down, or top to bottom, then across).

3. Quick Print

On the Quick Access toolbar, one of the commands you can add is called "Quick Print." (You can also add Print Preview.) Quick Print automatically sends your entire spreadsheet to the printer.

Page Layout

Many of the settings in the Print window are repeated on the ribbon under the Page Layout tab. Headers and Footers are located on the Insert tab of the ribbon, or accessed through the View Page, or (as described above) created through the Print Preview Page Setup screen.

1. Themes

Themes control the "look" of your document (they work in Word, Excel, PowerPoint, and Access). Built-in themes create a "Theme Design," identified by a name, such as "Office" or "Facet." You can, of course, create your own themes, which becomes an important step of "branding" (creating *your* look).

There are three parts to a theme design, each identified by the same name as the overall design:

- *Colors*—Selects the colors that become used in all text, fills, backgrounds, charts, shapes, etc.
- *Fonts*—Defines the default or built-in font for an entire document.
- *Effects*—Picks particular design effects (such as drop-shadows or bevels or glows) that are used by Excel's building choices.

On each item's dropdown is the "Customize" option, which lets you create your own. If you save your customized choices, they are then added to the Themes list for future use, and they also become available in all Microsoft Office programs.

2. Page Setup

Most of these options are repeated under the Print Preview Page Setup window (discussed above). They include the settings for your print margins, paper orientation (portrait or landscape), paper size, print area (how much of your document to print), page print breaks (force an area to start on a new page), background (insert a background image behind your spreadsheet, as a watermark), and print titles (rows or columns of your table that you would like to repeat at the top or the left of multiple pages).

3. Other Page Options

- *Scale to Fit*—Adjusts your worksheet to fit on the paper; it allows you to enlarge or to shrink.
- *Sheet Options*—Controls both the View and the Print settings for gridlines (do you want to see them on your screen? Do you want to print them?) and the column and row headings.
- *Arrange*—Controls how graphics, pictures, and other objects are positioned on your page (bring forward in front, or send back behind).

Note that if you use the Insert tab on the ruler to insert your Headers and Footers, your screen view shifts to Page Layout (as opposed to Normal, in the View toolbar in the lower right corner of your Excel screen). You'll see a new tab on the ribbon for "Header & Footer Tools / Design." It will include all the choices for what you can have in a header or footer, including page number, page count, date and time, file name and path, and sheet name.

Be sure to click the Normal view when done, if you want to return to the standard Excel screen.

Data Tools

1. Sort

There are multiple ways to sort in Excel. There are simple A-Z and Z-A sorts on the Home tab as well as on the Data tab of the ribbon; if you elect to use either of these commands, make sure you highlight *all* the data to be sorted. To alphabetize by the first column of the highlighted area, you can use the A-to-Z button on the ribbon. *Warning!* If you have three columns of information to be sorted, but you highlight only the first column, then only that data will be rearranged—not the other columns. If this happens, remember to use Edit/Undo to reverse your last step.

If you wish to sort by some other column in the highlighted area, or if you wish to sort by multiple columns (such as Last Name *and* First Name), use the dropdown on the Sort button and select "Custom Sort." This window (Figure 12), lets you select which column(s) to sort by, allowing you to add multiple sort levels. Be sure to specify whether or not your data have headers (a title row, which you would *not* want to sort).

Figure 15 - Custom Sort

Although Excel is *not* a database (Microsoft Access is), it does provide some easy-to-use database features. Databases are all about *information management* and what you can do with that information. Most the Excel's database features are on the Data tab of the ribbon.

To better understand databases operations, here's a simple model:

First	Last	Age	Income	Gender
Fred	Smith	42	$35,000	M
Sally	Sampson	67	$45,000	F
Joe	Smith	54	$72,000	M
Jane	Jones	33	$60,000	F

Figure 16 - Sample of Data

To understand databases, it's important to know about records and fields. A *record* is all the information pertaining to a person, place, thing—or whatever it is the database is tracking. Excel would call this a "row." So the row for Sally Sampson contains all the information pertaining to her and her alone. A *field* is the detail for the record. Excel would call this a column. For this sample database, the Fields are FIRST, LAST, AGE, INCOME, and GENDER. Here are some simple tasks you can do with a database:

- **Query or Find**—Seeking and locating records that meet specific requirements:
  Find all records for men (M)
      Fred and Joe
  Find all records for those older than 40 (>40)
      Fred, Sally, and Joe
- **Sort**—Arranging all the records in either ascending or descending order:
  List the records in alphabetical order, by last name
      Jane at the top, Fred at the bottom.
  List the records in descending order, by income
      Joe at the top, Fred at the bottom.

When creating a database, you need to have field headings in the first row, and don't skip a row before starting to input the data. The database must be contiguous (that means, no title across the top; if you need a title, put it in a header).

To Sort: Click in any record, it doesn't matter which one, but it must be under the field by which you want to sort. Then from the "Home" ribbon or from the "Data" ribbon, click the Custom Sort button.

2. Filter

Click on any cell in the database. Then select "Sort and Filter" from the "Home" ribbon, or choose "Filter" on the ribbon tab for Data. Notice that the field headings (first row) get dropdown-arrows to the right of each cell. Click on an arrow, such as the one next to Gender, and what appears are field contents of various records.

Figure 17 - Filter Turned On

If you unselect the checkmark next to "M" and click OK, the table will only show "F" while the filter is on.

First ▼	Last ▼	Age ▼	Incom ▼	Gende ▼
Sally	Sampson	67	$45,000	F
Jane	Jones	33	$60,000	F

Figure 18 - Filter of "F" (Female)

Important! To redisplay all the missing records, you must click on the same down arrow, then click "Select All." This will restore all hidden data. Or you can turn off Filter, which restores everything to original order.

To query for and display records for those age 40 and over, click on the "AGE" dropdown and select "Custom." A dialog box appears that displays the Field Heading. Below that is an equal sign. Select one of the logical operators <,>,=, etc. to specify the criteria for the search. In this case, you would want the operator "is greater than or equal to." In the neighboring box, type 40, then select OK. Only those records where the age is greater than 40 will be visible.

Filter Wildcard Characters

The purpose of wildcards are to provide flexibility in your matches. When you use the Filter dropdown and select "Custom," you can use wildcards to do "fill-in-the-blank" searches.

?	Any single character	Sm?th	matches Smith, Smyth, but not Smooth (which would require 2 ??)
*	Any characters	S*	matches Smith, Sampson, Sorenson, etc
#	Any numeric digit	5##	matches 500 to 599
[ ]	Any characters in bracket	Sm[iy]th	matches Smith or Smyth, but not Smoth
-	Any characters within the range (must be in brackets)	J[N-Z]nes	matches Jones but not Janes
!	Any characters except (must be in brackets)	[!N-Z]	excludes Jones but not Janes

For example, if you were given the list

Alabama
Atlanta
Atlantic City

Bahama
Jamaica
Chicago

and you filtered on a*, you would get Alabama, Atlanta, and Atlantic City (begins with a); if you did *a, you would get Alabama, Atlanta, Bahama, Jamaica (ends with a); a*a would match Alabama and Atlanta (begins and ends with a); and *a* would match all 6 locations (a anywhere).

3. Text to Columns

This command breaks text in one cell into separate cells, on the basis of a common character or symbol (such as comma or space). For example, suppose someone gives you a list of names and asks you to sort them, but they were typed in one column (not two), so the last name is not separate—which means you *cannot* sort by last name. "Text to Columns" will break the first name and last name into two columns (assuming you don't have any middle initials).

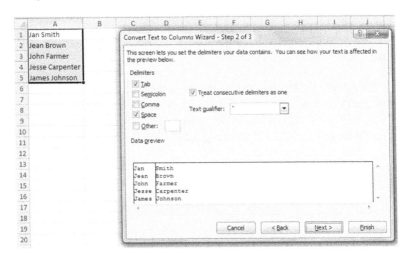

Figure 19 - Text to Columns

The Text to Columns Wizard begins by asking how your data is separated. There are two options: fixed width and delimited. Fixed width is more common with mainframe computers (not personal computers); it means that a certain number of spaces were left for each field (that is, first name might be 25, and if you're name is Tom or Ann, you still have 25 spaces). Most personal computers use delimited, which means there is a particular character or symbol separating the different kinds of information. This symbol might be a simple as a blank space; it very often is a comma (referred to as a Comma-Separated Value, or CSV). Other comma separators are semicolons and tabs. There is also an option to type in "Other" (such as * or _).

CSV files often have " " around the data, so be sure to have the "Text Qualifier" box checked on.

If you need to specify, the next step of the wizard gives you an opportunity to identify data as text, numbers, dates, etc.

If someone has a middle initial, or a prefix such as Mr. and Mrs. or suffice such as Jr., those have to be fixed manually, because each one may become a separate column.

4. Remove Duplicates and Consolidate

"Remove Duplicates" is a useful but dangerous tool. It does exactly what it says. It looks for identical data in columns that you specify (such as First Name and Last Name), and when they match, the rows are deleted.

I think this can be dangerous because it doesn't show you what it is going to delete—it just deletes it! So if you decide to use you, you might want to take some time to look through your data to make sure you don't have unexpected matches before committing yourself to the deleting.

"Consolidate" is similar, but it does *not* change the original data— it outputs to a new table. However, it is limited to operating on only two columns at a time. One column must contain the duplicates; the second column can be used to get a resulting total or average, count, standard deviation, etc. Here is a sample.

Elston Hardware	78.98
Elston Hardware	41.98
Dunkin' Donuts	56.96
VistaPrint	43.25
Home Depot	109.8
Home Depot	35.92
Home Depot	7.48
Home Depot	164.94

Figure 20 - Data to be Consolidated

To run a consolidation, first select the cells where you want the results to be positioned. Then click on the Consolidate button. This screen will appear:

Figure 21 - Consolidate

At the beginning is the Function (such as Sum) you wish to use. Below that is the "Reference" box—what is the area you are trying to consolidate? This is where you click, then highlight your two columns of data. If you want to run more than one consolidation (such as getting a sum, an average, and a count), be sure to select "Add," which stores the reference for re-use.

The key part is in the lower left corner, called "Use labels in." Where is your repetitive information? Across the top row, or down the left column? In this example, my repetition is in the left column. When I click OK, I get a new table that looks like this:

Elston Hardware	120.96
Dunkin' Donuts	56.96
VistaPrint	43.25
Home Depot	318.14

Figure 22 - Data after Consolidating

The resulting consolidation is a new table, and does not change or affect the original data (see Pivot Tables below for similar options). Each entry shows only once, and (since I had selected the Sum function), there is a total for each company. Data do not have to be sorted to use Consolidate; however, remember that you can only consolidate *two* columns at a time.

5. Data Validation

Data Validation allows you to control what kind of data is acceptable to be typed. Clicking the dropdown and selecting Data Validation brings up a window with a dropdown:

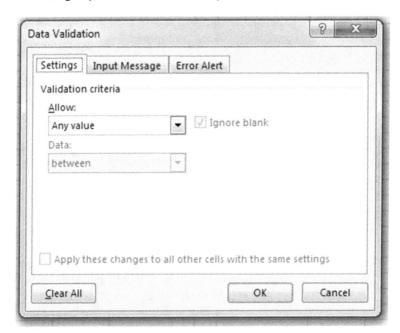

Figure 23 - Data Validation

On the dropdown you can select what can be typed—whole numbers, decimals, dates, etc. At the top are two additional tabs:

- *Input Message*—this allows you to type a little screen prompt reminding the typist what he or she can enter
- *Error Alert*—what if they type something that is not acceptable? There needs to be an error message. What would you like it to say? Here you can type your own error messages.

6. What-If Analysis

Scenarios

Scenarios are very useful when you want to store multiple numbers in the same cells, and then select which set of numbers to display at a given time. This is used frequently by people who work with budgets, and want to show the budget based on varying assumptions.

You have a worksheet that displays this year's sales figures. You need to predict next year's sales, based on national economic indicators. But what if those figures change, up *or* down? You can create scenarios based on how these indicators vary and will give different answers.

To create a scenario within a spreadsheet, first enter the base set of numbers you want to work with (the starting point). Highlight the area that you want to be able to create the scenario for, then go to the "Data" tab on the ribbon and click the dropdown for "What-If Analysis." One of your choices is the "Scenario Manager." Start by clicking the "Add" button to create your first scenario; you must assign a unique name to it, and confirm the values.

Figure 24 - Scenario Manager

Once the starting scenario exists, click "Add" again and create a new set of values. Continue this process of "adding" scenarios until you have as many versions as you need.

At the bottom of the scenario manager is the "Show" button, which allows you to select which scenario to show at any time. Only one can be shown at any given time.

If you wish to show all your scenarios at once, then use the "Summary" button, which will create a new table of all your values.

Scenario Summary				
	Current Values:	Start	Cuts	Overtime
Changing Cells:				
$B$26	35.0	35.0	20.0	40.0
$B$27	37.5	37.5	20.0	40.0
$B$28	40.0	40.0	25.0	45.0
$B$29	25.0	25.0	15.0	30.0
Result Cells:				
$B$30	137.5	137.5	80.0	155.0

Notes: Current Values column represents values of changing cells at time Scenario Summary Report was created. Changing cells for each scenario are highlighted in gray.

Figure 25 - 3 Scenarios, Summary View

At any time, you can go back to the Scenario Manager and show a different scenario, and also add, delete, or edit scenarios. (The "Merge" command lets you pull scenarios from other sheets.)

Goal Seek

The Goal Seek command on the Data ribbon is like a reverse formula. You know the answer you need, but you don't know what numbers will get you to that answer. Excel will calculate the necessary value for you, and ask if you want to use it. The only requirement is that the resulting answer *must* be based on a formula or function.

As an example, let's suppose you wanted to calculate mortgage payments with different interest rates, and see which interest rate would get your payment under $1,000 a month. You would be using the =PMT function (Financial library) to make the calculation. The PMT function requires several components to make its argument work:

- *Rate (Interest Rate):* The APR (Annual) must be divided by 12 to calculate monthly payments. Let's assume you have a current rate of 5.25%, and we'll divide in the PMT function.
- *Nper (Number of Payments):* 20 years or 30? Let's go with 30, so you have 360 payments.
- *Pv (Value of Mortgage):* Let's assume you have a $200,000 mortgage.

Using the =PMT function, you would find that your monthly payment would be $1,104.41. Your goal is to get that down to $999.00. The initial calculation would look like this (with Show Formulas on *and* off).

	A	B
1	Argument Requirements:	Value
2	Interest rate (/12, or monthly)	0.0525
3	Number of payments (length)	360
4	Amount of mortgage	200000
5		
6		
7	Monthly Payment:	=PMT(B2/12,B3,B4)
8		

	A	B
1	Argument Requirements:	Value
2	Interest rate (/12, or monthly)	5.25%
3	Number of payments (length)	360
4	Amount of mortgage	$ 200,000
5		
6		
7	Monthly Payment:	($1,104.41)
8		

Figure 26 - PMT Function for Mortgage Payment (Show Formulas "On" in the Top, "Off" in the Bottom)

Your goal is to reduce that monthly payment in B7. So click on B7, then go to Data/What-If Analysis and select Goal Seek. There will be three boxes to be filled out: which cell to change, change to what value, and do this by changing which cell that is used in the calculation.

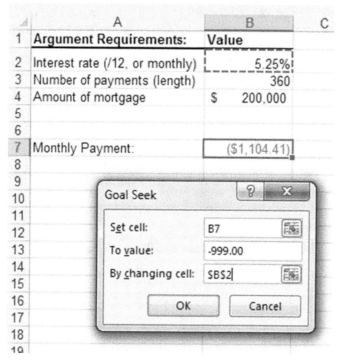

Figure 27 - Goal Seek Criteria

In this case, I am changing cell B7 (the monthly payment) to negative 999 (because it's a payment, not an income), by changing cell B2 (the percent rate). When you hit OK, the table recalculates, and Goal Seeks asks you to accept or cancel the result. When I hit OK, I see my new interest rate needs to be 4.38% to reach my goal.

	A	B
1	**Argument Requirements:**	Value
2	Interest rate (/12, or monthly)	4.38%
3	Number of payments (length)	360
4	Amount of mortgage	$ 200,000
5		
6		
7	Monthly Payment:	($999.00)
8		

Figure 28 - Same Table, After Goal Seek (New Interest Rate)

Subtotals and Group/Ungroup

If you have a large table with a lot of repetitive information, and you need to have totals, averages, or other basic results, there is a nifty feature in Excel called "Subtotal" that will automatically generate subtotals and grand totals for you (without you having to use functions).

The subtotal command looks for repetitive values and adds totals (or averages, counts, etc.) at each change in data. It also adds an outline toolbar called "Grouping" for viewing on the left side of the spreadsheet. Subtotals can also be removed when no longer needed (i.e., this feature can be turned on and off; it is temporary and does not permanently alter data). The *one requirement* is that your data must be sorted by the item for which you wish to get subtotals.

As an example, let's track employee absences for four staff members, who may have been sick or else taken some vacation time:

Staff	Hours Absent	Reason
Alice	5	Sick
Alice	2	Vacation
Alice	5	Vacation
Alice	4	Vacation
Bob	3	Sick
Bob	5	Vacation
Bob	4	Vacation
Bob	6.5	Sick
Bob	7.5	Sick
Carol	3	Vacation
Carol	7	Sick
Ted	6	Sick
Ted	7	Sick
Ted	5.5	Sick
Ted	2.5	Vacation

It might be useful to know a total "hours absent" for each employee, and a grand total for all absences. Since my data are sorted by staff, I can subtotal by staff:

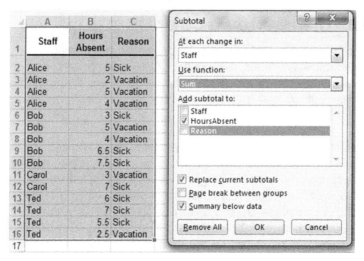

Figure 29 - Subtotal Dialog Window

At the top of the Subtotal window is a dropdown where you indicate what you are calculating on. Since my first column is Staff, the default becomes Staff. The second line is what calculation you are trying to use: sum, count, average, standard deviation, etc. The third part is which column are you calculating; I've selected Hours Absent. Then I hit OK.

	A	B	C
1	Staff	Hours Absent	Reason
2	Alice	5	Sick
3	Alice	2	Vacation
4	Alice	5	Vacation
5	Alice	4	Vacation
6	**Alice Total**	16	
7	Bob	3	Sick
8	Bob	5	Vacation
9	Bob	4	Vacation
10	Bob	6.5	Sick
11	Bob	7.5	Sick
12	**Bob Total**	26	
13	Carol	3	Vacation
14	Carol	7	Sick
15	**Carol Total**	10	
16	Ted	6	Sick
17	Ted	7	Sick
18	Ted	5.5	Sick
19	Ted	2.5	Vacation
20	**Ted Total**	21	
21	**Grand Total**	73	

Figure 30 - Result of Subtotal Command

At each change in "Staff," there is not a subtotal. At the bottom is a grand total. On the left side is the "Grouping," where I can collapse or expand each section. Across the upper left are 3 numbers, indicating I have 3 levels of information. If I click the 2, I see only the second level:

		Staff	Hours Absent	Reason
+	6	Alice Total	16	
+	12	Bob Total	26	
+	15	Carol Total	10	
+	20	Ted Total	21	
−	21	Grand Total	73	

Figure 31 - Grouped Data

I can then go back to the Subtotal command and click "Remove All," and my original table returns. Perhaps I now need to know totals by Reason (were they sick or on vacation?). Then I need to sort by Reason (use the Custom Sort so you can select the third column), then re-use the Subtotal command.

		Staff	Hours Absent	Reason	
+	10			47.5	Sick Total
+	18			25.5	Vacation Total
−	19			73	Grand Total
	20				

Figure 32 - Subtotal by Reason

Pivot Tables

Pivot Tables are especially well-suited for taking enormous amounts of data and summarizing that data into useful reports. To rearrange the worksheet into a pivot table, you'll need to drag and drop column headings to specific locations on the pivot table window, and Microsoft Excel then crunches the data accordingly. Using the same data as we used in the Subtotal, let's design a table that tells us both how many hours each staff member was out *and* how many hours they were out for each reason.

To begin, you need raw data. The general rule is you need at least three columns to create a proper pivot table. One column becomes row headers; one column becomes column headers, and one column usually contains the data to be summarized. (You can of course have more than three columns, and have subcategories within your pivot table.)

1. Create a PivotTable

To create a Pivot Table, select a cell anywhere in the data area, and then click the Insert tab on the ribbon to find the Pivot Table command. This screen will ask you to select your data range (it usually does it automatically for you, but check to make sure it's doing it correctly), and it also wants to know where the new pivot table should be positioned (I usually prefer a New Worksheet, which is the default). So, essentially this is all already completed, so I just have to click OK. That takes us to the PivotTable1 screen, where the key part is the Pivot Table Fields on the right of your screen.

The Fields panel should show you your column headings from the original data. You then move each field to the designated areas: columns (headings across the top of your pivot table), row (headings at the left of the pivot table), and values (the data to be summed or analyzed). You can have multiple fields in each category. As you drag and drop these items into their respective areas, the resulting report is displayed. The next step is to further manipulate your data by rearranging fields on the table, or removing fields or adding fields (if you have more than 3 columns). This action is *pivoting* the data—what Pivot Tables are all about. You'll find that all duplicate entries have been consolidated, and the data automatically sorted.

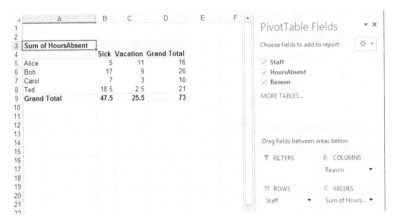

Figure 33 - Sample Pivot Table

Drag the fields to pivot the presentation. I'll reverse Reason and Staff:

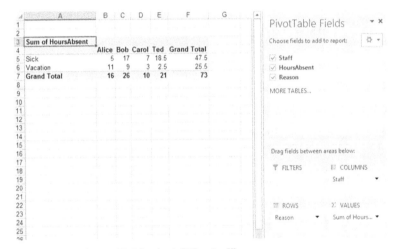

Figure 34 - Same Table, but "Pivoted"

I might even want to simplify my presentation, by dragging Staff below Reason (or Reason below Staff):

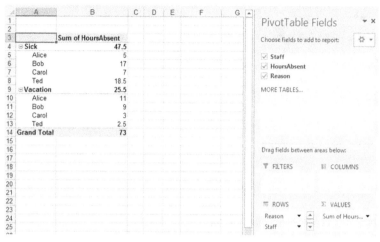

Figure 35 - Different Pivot Format

2. Modifying Reports

A Pivot Table can be modified to display different results such as averages, counts, minimums, maximums, etc. The Pivot Table "Values" dropdown allows you to change between sum, average, max, min, count, and more. (As with the Subtotals feature, text fields can only be summarized with the COUNT function.) Note that data *are* still linked to the original data table, but *do not* update automatically if you go back and change the original data; use the "Refresh" button on the ribbon to update data after changes.

3. Formatting

While in the Pivot Table, there are two new tables on the ribbon, called Analyze and design. Analyze contains your settings, but it also has a useful button called "Recommended Pivot Tables." These are simply pre-designed layouts you can pick from when formatting your pivot table.

Under Designs, Excel provides an assortment of formats to choose from. Simply choose a format, and your data is now more readable (or sometimes not). Additionally, these automatic formats are persistent formats, which means the table's formatting will hold even as you continue to pivot your data around by dragging and dropping additional fields on the screen.

4. Pivot Charts

The next step is to turn your Pivot Table into a chart. On the ribbon, under Analyze, click the Pivot Chart button to launch the chart screen, which then adds a chart to the table. Just as with Pivot Tables, Pivot Charts are interactive as well. Simply drag and drop the data onto the chart to see instant results. Let's use my original Pivot Table example and turn it into my favorite chart type, a stacked column chart.

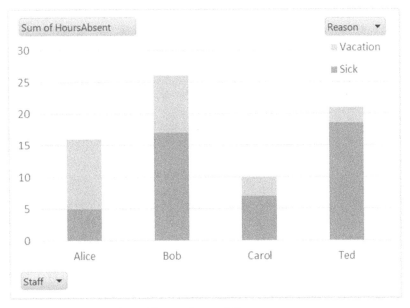

Figure 36 - Pivot Chart (from Figure 32)

Hm. Looks like Bob has really missed a lot of work. And I wonder why Ted has been getting sick so often? Maybe he needs to take more vacations.

More Functions

1. Date and Time Functions

Dates to Excel are actually numbers, where each subsequent day is accorded an increasing numerical value (Microsoft calendars start on 1/1/1900, which makes that numerical day 1). Here are some sample dates:

Date		Numeric value
Jan 1, 1900	=	1
Jan 2, 1900	=	2
Jan 1, 1901	=	366
Jan 1, 2000	=	36,526
Jan 1, 2014	=	41,640

This can be very useful in doing math calculations with dates. For example, if you are a doctor in a hospital who is tracking patients, you might find it helpful to chart "days of survival" or "days under treatment." If the patient started treatment on Sept. 14, 2007, and is still alive on October 1, 2011, that patient has "survived" 1,478 days:

$$="10/1/2011"-"9/14/2007"$$

Note the quote marks around the dates; this indicates they are treated as a unit (otherwise the / would be translated into a division command).

You might also want to calculate 90 days from today:

$$=TODAY()+90$$

If today happened to be February 5, 2014 (when I'm writing this), then the answer would be 5/6/2014. I used the =TODAY() function, so that it will update the answer each time I come back to the spreadsheet; alternatively, I could have just typed in a date +90: ="2/5/2014"+90 returns the same May 6, 2014.

Formatting the date cell is the process by which you can change the numeric appearance. On the Format button of the Ribbon, under the Number formats (on the dropdown in the lower corner), is a command called "Format Cells," which includes a Number tab with a "Custom" format option.

Day Code	Appearance	Month Code	Appearance	Year Code	Appearance
d	7	m	11	yy	09
dd	07	mm	11	yyy	2009
ddd	Tue	mmm	Nov		
dddd	Tuesday	mmmm	November		

Here's how you might manipulate the formatting codes to change the date's appearance:

Tuesday, November 7, 1995   dddd, mmmm d, yyy
7/11/95   d/m/y
Nov. 7, 1995   m. d, yyy

Time, to further this concept, is accorded a decimal value, where if one day equals the value of one (1), then:

6:00 am   .25
12:00 Noon   .5
6:00 PM   .75

Excel Tip: There are several functions built into Excel for working with time. If you need to calculate payroll, for example, you might want to use the =hour function to convert hours into number (for subtracting) and the =minute function to do the same to minutes. Using these two functions, you can turn 3:45 PM into the values 15 and 45.

2. Text Functions

Cleaning up sloppy typing can be frustrating. Suppose someone gave you a table to work on that looked like this:

first	last
bob	smith
ted	jones
carol	adams
alice	brown

You probably don't want to have to sit there and manually fix the capitalization. That's where Text functions can be very useful.

One of the best Text functions in Excel is called "Proper." It "properly" capitalizes the beginning of words. If you had "jan smith" in a cell A1, the function =proper(A1) would give you "Jan Smith." There are also functions called "upper" (for all upper-case) and "lower" (for all lower-case), which work exactly the same way.

It's important to understand that Proper does *not* change what is already typed. It's a function, so it results in a new column that contains the function—not text. In this example, the top part is what you would see or print, but the second part is the actual content.

⊿	A	B	C	D
1	first	last	First	Last
2	bob	smith	Bob	Smith
3	ted	jones	Ted	Jones
4	carol	adams	Carol	Adams
5	alice	brown	Alice	Brown
6				
7	first	last	=PROPER(A7)	=PROPER(B7:B11)
8	bob	smith	=PROPER(A8)	=PROPER(B8:B12)
9	ted	jones	=PROPER(A9)	=PROPER(B9:B13)
10	carol	adams	=PROPER(A10)	=PROPER(B10:B14)
11	alice	brown	=PROPER(A11)	=PROPER(B11:B15)
12				

Figure 37 - Corrected Text Using Proper

Suppose you then wanted to take the first name and last name and combine them into a real name, or even put the last name first and add a comma (i.e, "Smith, Bob"). The function to do that is called "Concatenate." Often referred to as a "string" function, this command joins cells. If you had "Jan" in cell A1, and "Smith" in cell B1, you could use concatenate to put them together. For example, =concatenate(B1,", ",A1) would give you "Smith, Jan." (Note the ", " indicates text to be inserted between B1 and A1.) Here's the same data concatenated (top half is what prints, bottom half shows the function).

	A	B	C	D	E
1	first	last	First	Last	Last, First
2	bob	smith	Bob	Smith	Smith, Bob
3	ted	jones	Ted	Jones	Jones, Ted
4	carol	adams	Carol	Adams	Adams, Carol
5	alice	brown	Alice	Brown	Brown, Alice
6					
7	first	last	=PROPER(A7)	=PROPER(B7:B11)	=CONCATENATE(D7,", ",C7)
8	bob	smith	=PROPER(A8)	=PROPER(B8:B12)	=CONCATENATE(D8,", ",C8)
9	ted	jones	=PROPER(A9)	=PROPER(B9:B13)	=CONCATENATE(D9,", ",C9)
10	carol	adams	=PROPER(A10)	=PROPER(B10:B14)	=CONCATENATE(D10,", ",C10)
11	alice	brown	=PROPER(A11)	=PROPER(B11:B15)	=CONCATENATE(D11,", ",C11)
12					

Figure 38 - Concatenated Names

When you have finished "properizing" and "concatenating" your names, you might like to turn the resulting functions back in to text. Remember "paste special" (on page 21)? That's where we found Paste Links. But there is another very useful option on there called "Paste Values." This command converts functions and for-mulas into actual text or number content. It only works when you copy (not cut), and you must Paste Special to a new area (not back on top of what you copied).

Other Text Functions

Left or *Right*—These functions trim text, from the left side or the right side. For example, if you had a cell A1 with Social Security numbers, and you only wanted to use the last four digits, you would use =right(a1,4).

255-48-5478	=RIGHT(N1,4)	5478
943-28-3718	=RIGHT(N2,4)	3718
582-02-9287	=RIGHT(N3,4)	9287

Figure 39 - "Right" Function

Len—How many characters does a cell contain (length)? In a cell A1 that contains "Chicago," =len(a1) would show 7.

3. VLookup and HLookup

You can use the Vlookup function to search for a particular value in the first column of a range of cells (called the "Table Array"), and then return a value from another cell on that same row of the table. For example, suppose you work in a paint factory, and you have to invoice clients for paint orders. You have a "Table Array" that identifies each product with a bar code, spells out its title, and shows the price; this is your "Table Array."

	A	B	C
1	Barcode	Paint	Price
2	1000	White	$ 15.97
3	2000	Black	$ 18.38
4	3000	Red	$ 24.19
5	4000	Orange	$ 22.70
6	5000	Yellow	$ 18.97
7	6000	Green	$ 19.35
8	7000	Blue	$ 25.73
9	8000	Indigo	$ 27.38
10	9000	Violet	$ 29.30

Figure 40 - Sample "Table Array" for a Lookup

You also have a list of orders, along with the barcodes of the paint they would like to have; you want Excel to look up the barcode and return the appropriate product name and price (note the barcodes are not exact matches with the Table Array; each barcode represents a range of products—everything from 1000 to 1999 is a white paint; everything from 2000 to 2999 is a black paint; 1897 is a type of white, 2948 is a type of black).

E	F	G	H
Orders:	Barcode	Paint	Price
Jane	1897		
Jim	5837		
Joan	8573		
June	5326		
Julie	2948		
Jesse	3015		
James	9234		
Jean	4218		
Joanne	1057		
Jed	5271		
Juan	7285		

Figure 41 - Data to be "Looked Up"

If you know the order's barcode number, you can use the Vlookup function to return either the name of the paint or the price of that paint to your Orders table. (Note you have to do each column separately.)

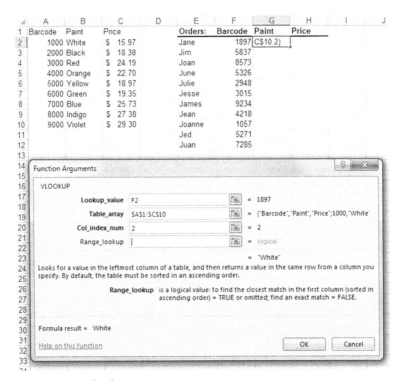

Figure 42 - Vlookup Arguments

In this example, the Lookup_value is the barcode in cell F2 of the Orders. The Table_array is A1:C10, but the cells must be locked (made absolute, by using F4) so the function can be filled down. The Col_index_num is 2 because I want to see the name of the paint, which is stored in the second column of the Table array. Range_lookup is blank; if I put in the argument False, then there must be an exact match for the answer to appear, otherwise Excel looks for the closest match in ascending numerical order.

The resulting function is =vlookup(F2,$A$1:$C$10,2) . To find the paint price, the function is =vlookup(F2,$A$1:$C$10,3) .

My resulting table, once I've filled the functions down through Juan, would look like this:

	A	B	C	D	E	F	G	H
1	Barcode	Paint	Price		Orders:	Barcode	Paint	Price
2	1000	White	15.97		Jane	1897	=VLOOKUP(F2,$A$1:$C$10,2)	=VLOOKUP(F2,$A$1:$C$10,3)
3	2000	Black	18.38		Jim	5837	=VLOOKUP(F3,$A$1:$C$10,2)	=VLOOKUP(F3,$A$1:$C$10,3)
4	3000	Red	24.19		Joan	8573	=VLOOKUP(F4,$A$1:$C$10,2)	=VLOOKUP(F4,$A$1:$C$10,3)
5	4000	Orange	22.7		June	5326	=VLOOKUP(F5,$A$1:$C$10,2)	=VLOOKUP(F5,$A$1:$C$10,3)
6	5000	Yellow	18.97		Julie	2948	=VLOOKUP(F6,$A$1:$C$10,2)	=VLOOKUP(F6,$A$1:$C$10,3)
7	6000	Green	19.35		Jesse	3015	=VLOOKUP(F7,$A$1:$C$10,2)	=VLOOKUP(F7,$A$1:$C$10,3)
8	7000	Blue	25.73		James	9234	=VLOOKUP(F8,$A$1:$C$10,2)	=VLOOKUP(F8,$A$1:$C$10,3)
9	8000	Indigo	27.38		Jean	4218	=VLOOKUP(F9,$A$1:$C$10,2)	=VLOOKUP(F9,$A$1:$C$10,3)
10	9000	Violet	29.3		Joanne	1057	=VLOOKUP(F10,$A$1:$C$10,2)	=VLOOKUP(F10,$A$1:$C$10,3)
11					Jed	5271	=VLOOKUP(F11,$A$1:$C$10,2)	=VLOOKUP(F11,$A$1:$C$10,3)
12					Juan	7285	=VLOOKUP(F12,$A$1:$C$10,2)	=VLOOKUP(F12,$A$1:$C$10,3)

	A	B	C	D	E	F	G	H
1	Barcode	Paint	Price		Orders:	Barcode	Paint	Price
2	1000	White	$ 15.97		Jane	1897	White	$ 15.97
3	2000	Black	$ 18.38		Jim	5837	Yellow	$ 18.97
4	3000	Red	$ 24.19		Joan	8573	Indigo	$ 27.38
5	4000	Orange	$ 22.70		June	5326	Yellow	$ 18.97
6	5000	Yellow	$ 18.97		Julie	2948	Black	$ 18.38
7	6000	Green	$ 19.35		Jesse	3015	Red	$ 24.19
8	7000	Blue	$ 25.73		James	9234	Violet	$ 29.30
9	8000	Indigo	$ 27.38		Jean	4218	Orange	$ 22.70
10	9000	Violet	$ 29.30		Joanne	1057	White	$ 15.97
11					Jed	5271	Yellow	$ 18.97
12					Juan	7285	Blue	$ 25.73

Figure 43 - Completed Vlookup

The V in Vlookup stands for vertical. Use Hlookup when your values are located in rows across the top of a data table, and you want to look down a specified number of rows. Use Vlookup when your comparison values are located in a column to the left of the data you want to find.

4. Logical Functions

The most-used Logical function in Excel is called "If." You constantly hear people talking about If-statements. "If" is a conditional result, where you specify the criteria (> or < or =) and the results if true and if false. It begins with a "Logical_test", such as a1>20. It is followed by a "Value_if_true" and a "Value_if_false."

	A	B	C
1	15.97	=IF(A1>20,"Out of stock","Order is on the way")	Order is on the way
2	18.97	=IF(A2>20,"Out of stock","Order is on the way")	Order is on the way
3	27.38	=IF(A3>20,"Out of stock","Order is on the way")	Out of stock
4	18.97	=IF(A4>20,"Out of stock","Order is on the way")	Order is on the way
5	18.38	=IF(A5>20,"Out of stock","Order is on the way")	Order is on the way

Figure 44 - If Function, Where Column C Is the Result

Protecting a Worksheet

"Protection" allows you to lock cells from the possibility that some-one might change the contents. Protection also allows you to "hide" the cell function or formula—the answer will appear in the cell, but the formula bar is empty. "Protection" is located on any of the Home expanded dialog boxes (such as for Font or Align-ment), where there is a tab for Protection.

Note that cells are automatically locked—but "protection" is not activated. The first step in protecting a worksheet is to "unlock" the cells you want to be editable (where people can make changes). Uncheck the "Locked" checkbox to make cells editable; put a check in the "Hidden" checkbox if you want to hide your formulas and functions on the Formula bar.

Once you have unlocked the cells, you can then "protect" the sheet. This command is located on the "Review" tab of the ruler. You have an option to assign a password for unprotecting, so other users cannot bypass your lock without the password. You probably want to uncheck the box that says "Select locked cells"—users probably shouldn't click protected cells, since they can't work in them. Make sure you have a check in "Select unlocked cells," so users can make changes in the areas you have made editable.

Once you OK the "Protect Sheet" command, you can no longer click in cells *except* those that were unlocked. You cannot make other cells editable unless you know the password (and if you for-get your password, Microsoft will *not* help you!).

Excel Keyboard Shortcuts

Move to cell "A1" .... Ctrl+Home
Move to "A" Column of worksheet .... Home
Go To F5
Move to end or start of table or worksheet ... End+arrow; Ctrl+End
Move one window Up/Down .... Page Up/Pg Down
Move one window Left/Right .... Alt+Pg Up/Alt+Pg Down
Move to next sheet .... Ctrl+Pg Down
Insert AutoSum .... ALT+=
Select entire Column .... CTRL+Spacebar
Select entire Row .... SHFT+Spacebar
Clear Cell Contents .... Delete
Clear Cell Contents, and Edit .... Backspace
Absolute Cell Reference ($) F4
Show Values/Show Formulas .... CTRL+`(left quote ~)
Edit a Cell's Data F2
Edit a Cell's Contents (data, notes, etc.) .... CTRL+F2
Format Cells .... Ctrl+1
Insert Cells .... Ctrl+SHIFT+=

Other Keyboard Shortcuts

Save .... CTRL-S
New .... CTRL-N
Open .... CTRL-O
Print .... CTRL-P
Select All .... CTRL-A
Undo last action .... CTRL-Z
Redo last action .... CTRL-Y
Cut .... CTRL-X
Copy .... CTRL-C
Paste .... CTRL-V
Find .... CTRL-F
Find & Replace .... CTRL-H
Fill Down .... CTRL-D
Fill Right .... CTRL-R
Help F1
Bold .... CTRL-B
Italics .... CTRL-I
Underline .... CTRL-U
Ribbon .... ALT

Index of Key Terms

Absolute cell 19
Centering across columns 9
Chart 23
Concatenate 54
Conditional formatting 9
Consolidate 38
Data validation 40
Date 52
Document 11
File 3, 10, 11, 27
Fill 5, 9, 12, 19, 60
Filter 35
Formatting 8
Formula 2, 3, 4, 5, 7, 12, 13, 16, 19, 21, 42, 59
Formula auditing 16
Formula bar 3, 4, 5, 7, 59
Function 2, 13, 14, 15, 16, 40, 42, 43, 50, 52, 53, 54, 56, 57, 58, 59
Function library 14
Goal seek 42
Group 45
Headers 28
Highlighting 6
If 58
Keyboard 5
Links 20, 55
Margins 28
Mouse 5
Nesting 12
Noncontiguous ranges 6
Numeric keypad 7
Page setup 27, 29, 31
Paste special 21, 22, 55
Pemdas 2, 12
Pivot charts 51
Pivot tables 40, 48, 50, 51
Print 10, 11, 27, 28, 29, 30, 31, 32, 60
Print area 29
Protecting a worksheet 59

Remove duplicates 38
Ribbon 3
Right mouse button 10
Save 10
Saves the current document 10
Scale to fit 32
Scenarios 41
Shortcuts 60
Show formulas 16, 17, 21, 43
Sort 33
Sparklines 26
Spreadsheet 1, 4, 5, 11, 25, 26, 27, 30, 31, 41, 45, 52
Subtotals 45
Sum 13
Text functions 53
Text to columns 37
Vlookup 56
Wildcard 36

www.ingramcontent.com/pod-product-compliance
Lightning Source LLC
LaVergne TN
LVHW052312060326
832902LV00021B/3852